HOW THE GOSPEL SETS US FREE

How the Gospel Sets Us Free

Transforming Truths from Galatians

Erwin W. Lutzer

Moody Church Media
Chicago

Cover by Bryan Butler

HOW THE GOSPEL SETS US FREE

Published by Moody Church Media
Chicago, Illinois 60614
www.moodymedia.org

ISBN: 978-1-7942-3356-0

CONTENTS

CHAPTER 1

DISTORTING THE GOOD NEWS

Some time ago, I received a letter from a concerned religious leader who told me that he had received a personal revelation from the Lord Jesus Christ. He claimed Christ appeared to him and said, "My body is broken...please heal my body...I want my body to become one again." The letter went on to say that it was time that we minimized our differences as Christians and united around the doctrine of Christ. Catholics, Protestants, and various other Christian groups should confess the sin of division and come together to fulfill Christ's prayer for unity.

What do you think of such a revelation? Can all of Christendom be unified without compromising the gospel? Unfortunately, two very divergent answers are still given to the fundamental question of how a sinner can stand before a holy God.

Paul began Galatians with only a short greeting because something more important was on his mind:

this congregation was being pulled away into a distorted view of the Gospel of Christ. He chided them for mixing error with truth. “I am astonished that you are so quickly deserting him who called you in the grace of Christ and are turning to a different gospel—not that there is another one, but there are some who trouble you and want to distort the gospel of Christ” (Galatians 1:6–7).

How do we recognize a distortion of the gospel? Basically it comes down to this: all attempts to mix grace and works dilute the purity of the Christian message. Let’s rewind and look at three examples from church history.

DISTORTIONS OF THE GOSPEL

The first distortion began in the early centuries as sacramentalism grew within the church. The sacraments came to be viewed as having such intrinsic value that the worshippers did not even need to have a spiritual disposition or a change of heart to benefit from their power. These ordinances were not merely symbols, but actual means of grace given to those who were faithful to the teachings of the church. No one sacrament was sufficient, but perhaps if all of them were appropriated, the worshippers would receive enough grace to enter heaven. Salvation was not in the hands of God, it was in the hands of men; the priests could dispense or withhold these blessings as they wished.

Of course a problem arose: how much grace did one

need in order for God to be pleased? No one was sure.

Mysticism was a second distortion of the gospel. The soul, it was believed, was created by God and must reunite itself with God through contemplation. Many people retreated into monasteries to pursue a life of meditation and self-denial. They hoped to purify their souls so that they could approach God for themselves.

Once again a question arose: how much self-denial is really needed for the salvation of the soul? What if the soul is not entirely pure despite the disciplined efforts of the faithful?

Salvation, if it could be attained at all, was out of the reach of the common man. Not everyone had the time to devote his life to inner contemplation; not everyone was able to find satisfaction in having his soul somehow absorbed into the "being" of God.

A third distortion also developed. If one could perform at least one perfect act of contrition, one's soul was worthy of grace. But those who were honest admitted that all of their motives were mixed. Little wonder the church concluded that only a few ever exhibited this perfect act; only some select saints loved God perfectly!

Given these distorted ways of salvation, we all have to admit that we come up woefully short. If salvation depended 95% on God and 5% on me, my performance, my contemplation, or my pure motives—my eternal salvation is surely in jeopardy. Salvation, under these conditions, is always just a distant hope. No one can be sure.

Thankfully, the three distortions I have mentioned are not the gospel. There is a gulf as wide as the Grand Canyon between these beliefs and what the New Testament actually teaches. The difference is as great as heaven and hell. Little wonder Paul wrote, "But even if we or an angel from heaven should preach to you a gospel contrary to the one we preached to you, let him be accursed. As we have said before, so now I say again: If anyone is preaching to you a gospel contrary to the one you received, let him be accursed" (Galatians 1:8–9).

Regrettably, some men, such as Joseph Smith, did not take this warning seriously. Smith accepted false teaching from an "angel" and founded Mormonism which has misled millions. If he had read Paul's words, he would have known that angels cannot be trusted. The reason is obvious: there are two different kinds of angels that roam this planet, and often the evil ones appear as good in order to deceive us.

Paul condemns any false teachers who try to mix Law and grace; he is in direct opposition to those who think that faith in Christ *plus* some other work—some other ritual or revelation—is necessary for salvation.

THE TRUE GOSPEL

What then is the *true* gospel Paul preached? First of all, it teaches that *all human goodness is tainted.* Just as you can add billions of bananas and never get an orange, so all human goodness added together can never save a single sinner. All perfect acts of contrition, all attempts to find God within the soul, or all attempts to combine any good works with God's grace—all such theories lead to despair. The smallest speck of sin would keep us out of heaven.

Second, the true gospel affirms that *God accepts only what Christ did, not what we do.* His was the only perfect act of contrition. He alone had the purity of God, for He was, Himself, divine. Therefore, He did for us what we cannot do for ourselves.

Isn't it foolish to think that there is something we can do that will mean more to God than the work of His blessed Son? What arrogance to think that we can contribute to Christ's work through the sacraments, or our own meditations and tainted attempts to love the Almighty!

Third, the true gospel says that *there is one requirement: trust and faith in Christ.* The faith need not be great; Christ said that if we have "faith the size of a mustard seed" (Matthew 17:20 NASB), we can enter into the Kingdom of Heaven. But that faith must be directed only to Christ. Faith, even great faith, will not save us if it is in Christ *plus* ourselves or anything else. Faith the size of a mountain will damn us if it is placed in the sacraments or our own attempts to earn heaven our way.

We are saved by faith in Christ alone, and even that faith is a gift of God. He must give us the ability to receive the free gift! No wonder the Scriptures teach that "Salvation belongs to the LORD!" (Jonah 2:9b).

Now we can understand why a sinner can be accepted by God: it is because God receives sinners wholly on the basis of His blessed Son. Neither their *past*—good or bad—nor their *present* determines whether they will be welcomed into heaven. Ultimately, it is faith in Christ, and in Him alone, that determines the final outcome.

IMPLICATIONS OF THE GOSPEL

Now that we understand the basic aspects of the gospel, several implications follow.

First, God can save "big" sinners as easily as "small" ones. It is better that we be good citizens rather than wanton law breakers. But as far as God is concerned, since salvation is a free gift, no sin is too great for Him to forgive. No sinner has sunk so deeply but that God's grace and love is deeper still.

If you were giving $1,000 to select individuals, it would not make much difference whether they were rich or poor, black or white, decent citizens or criminals—your gift can be received by them all. Christ said that the prostitutes will go into the Kingdom of Heaven sooner than the self-righteous Pharisees who still think that their eternal destiny is somehow determined by their own noble efforts.

Second, we need the good news of the gospel every day. Although we are saved at the point in time when we personally trust Christ as Savior, we must come back to the gospel again and again. Only then do we silence our conscience and experience freedom in Christ.

Recently, I spoke to a man who ruined his marriage because of a sexual affair. He is now divorced and remarried; his sin had a devastating impact on two families. How can he, as a Christian, live with himself? What should people do when their sin has devastated the lives of others and there is no way to make it right? How can he wake up in the morning and live through the day?

Many people respond to such guilt by (1) trying to minimize their sin, emphasizing that there are other sinners in the world who are far worse than they. Of course that doesn't work because we know intuitively, regardless of what others have done, it is our sin that weighs so heavily on our shoulders. Or (2), others exaggerate their strong points, trying to balance the scales. But that doesn't work either, and it most assuredly does not impress God.

What is the scriptural answer? It is to admit that the truth about ourselves is terrible; in fact, it is far worse than we are willing to believe. But then we point to Christ and know that we are accepted in Him.

I need no other argument,
I need no other plea,
It is enough that Jesus died,
And that He died for me.

—"My Faith Has Found A Resting Place"
by E.E. Hewitt (Lidie H. Edmunds)

Should we bring together all of Christendom under one banner in the interest of unity? Should we assume that "because everyone believes in Christ" that we must unite the body of Christ because it is broken? I think not. Multitudes who believe in Christ will be lost forever for the simple reason that they believe in Christ *and* something else.

So, how shall I respond to the person who claims to have had a revelation from Christ saying we must unite? I reply as did Paul, "But even if we or an angel from heaven should preach to you a gospel contrary to the one we preached to you, let him be accursed" (Galatians 1:8).

CHAPTER 2

DEFENDING THE GOOD NEWS

Peter Marshall tells the story about a town in Europe that sat at the foot of a great mountain range. High up in the hills above the village, an old man served as the keeper of the springs. He patrolled the mountainside and made sure that the spring which fed the village below was always clear of silt, leaves, and dead animals.

Each day, the water would tumble down to the town below, cold and pure. Gardens were refreshed, lawns were green, and people had their thirst quenched. Summer and winter, the townspeople drank from its coolness and washed in its freshness.

But the town faced a crisis. Times were hard and the council had a budget to cut. Someone noticed a small amount of money committed to the salary of the keeper of the springs. They decided that they would release him of his duties and end his salary because most people seldom saw him, they didn't know who he was. They also theorized that the water would probably stay just as pure without this unknown guardian.

For the first few weeks, the water seemed to be the same, clear and pure. But gradually a green scum developed on its surface and leaves clogged with dirt and debris floated on top of the water. After a while, sickness came to the village and soon an epidemic raged, reaching into every home.

The town council met again in an emergency session. They realized they had made a bad decision, so they appointed a delegation to climb up into the mountains, find the old man, and beg him to resume his former labors. Before long, pure water flowed down to the village again; children laughed and played on the banks of the stream as they had in days gone by.

The Apostle Paul saw himself as standing at the head of a fountain, the "keeper of the spring" of the gospel message. He knew that if this water was diluted, contaminated, or otherwise made impure, the eternal destiny of millions of people would be affected.

The book of Galatians was written to keep the gospel from contamination. It is, perhaps, one of the earliest books of the New Testament, likely written in about AD 50. Already then, Paul had to fight against distortions of the gospel. Any addition to the Good News, any belief that circumcision was required along with faith in Christ in order to be saved, or any thought that the Law must be kept along with believing in the cross—Paul knew that all such teaching muddied the pure water of God's infinite grace.

In effect, Paul forever exposes the lie that human effort must be a part of the divine initiative in salvation. We've already learned that if salvation were 95% of God and 5% of man, our soul would be in jeopardy.

Paul defends his understanding of the gospel in three different ways.

THE GOSPEL'S ORIGIN

First, he argues that the gospel originated with God who revealed it to him. "For I would have you know, brothers, that the gospel that was preached by me is not man's gospel. For I did not receive it from any man, nor was I taught it, but I received it through a revelation of Jesus Christ" (Galatians 1:11–12).

The purity of this message is guaranteed by God Himself. Paul received it, he says, by revelation when he spent three years in Arabia after his conversion. Recall that prior to his conversion, he was entrenched in Judaism, a hater of Christians, and yet, he believed that he was righteous. No one could deny his dramatic conversion; and now, he appeals to it to authenticate his apostleship.

In Arabia, he probably studied the Old Testament and saw how it points toward Christ, the One he had come to know as Messiah. There, he also conversed with Christ and received the special message of the gospel. Needless to say, Paul's understanding of the gospel agreed completely with what Christ, Himself, taught.

THE PRACTICE OF THE GOSPEL

Second, Paul defends the practice of the gospel. When he came to the city of Antioch, he faced the uncomfortable responsibility of rebuking the famous apostle, Peter, for diluting the Christian message.

Here's what happened: Peter, who is generally believed to be the first among the apostles and is regarded by some as the first pope, began to waver. He would not eat with Gentiles, giving the impression that the gospel was not for them after all. His actions implied that Gentiles would have to become Jews in order to be saved. He feared the false teachers, so he held himself aloof, giving the impression that he was siding with these Judaizers.

How did Paul handle this wavering attitude? We read, "But when Cephas came to Antioch, I opposed him to his face, because he stood condemned" (Galatians 2:11). Paul did not deal with Peter in a back room. Because Peter's actions were public, the rebuke was public.

All distinctions based on ethnic origin, race, etc. have no place at the foot of the cross. Segregated churches are a perversion of the gospel. We are born equally separated from God, and when we are saved, we are equally brought near to God through faith.

Think of this remarkable incident. Paul's public rebuke of Peter is, in effect, saying that Peter was distorting the gospel without saying a word. Peter didn't say that the gospel was not for Gentiles, but by his actions alone, by withdrawing from the Gentiles, he was implying that it was so. For Paul, excluding anyone from God's grace deserved a stern public rebuke and humiliation!

THE MEANING OF THE GOSPEL

Third, Paul discusses what justification really means. "Yet we know that a person is not justified by works of the law but through faith in Jesus Christ, so we also have believed in Christ Jesus, in order to be justified by faith in Christ and not by works of the law, because by works of the law no one will be justified" (Galatians 2:16).

What does Paul mean by justification? *It is an enduring act of God by which we are declared righteous in Christ.* Notice it is an act; it happens at a point in time. Just as we grow in the womb until our birth, it might take time for us to come to faith in Christ. But just as our physical birth happens in a moment in time, so does our second birth—we are immediately made members of God's family.

Notice also, it is an act of *God;* it is not the work of a minister or a priest. After all, if we were not acquitted by

God, the word of anyone else would be irrelevant. Also, we are *declared righteous;* that is, justification is a declaration in heaven that we are just as righteous as Christ is. His righteousness is credited to us so that we are as approved by God as is Christ Himself.

Finally, it is an *enduring* act of God. We live our entire lives under the banner of God's matchless declaration. The perfect demands of God are always in force; He has never lowered His standards or chosen to ignore our sins. Every single day, God demands from me absolute perfection. I can only meet this obligation because Christ is my representative and is my righteousness before God.

This is why righteousness is not something I can grow into; it is not something that I can ever attain on my own. If I am to belong to God, He demands righteousness up front—it must be there in order for me to be brought into His presence as one of His children.

In John Bunyan's allegory, *The Pilgrim's Progress,* there is a man called Faithful who represents a Christian. He is tempted to marry three daughters of the world—the lust of the flesh, the lust of the eyes, and the pride of life. He resists the temptation but finds within his heart a tremendous desire to flirt with them. The question becomes, how can he handle these powerful impulses? How can a man who has been declared righteous by God find victory over the deeds of the flesh?

In the allegory, Moses, representing the Law, comes to beat him to death. Despite being declared righteous by God, the Law still condemns his own heart. So, Faithful tries to avert this sense of condemnation, but he can't do it by looking within himself or even by righteous living—important as that might be. He can only find freedom by returning to look at the hands of the crucified Savior.

The message of justification is this: *God has declared us righteous in Christ, therefore, we have total acceptance with Him legally*. But now we also have a means by which the guilt within our conscience can be taken away. The condemnation does not vanish when we consider our good deeds or attempt to rationalize why we should be free of this guilt. No, we are made free by looking outside of ourselves to Christ who has declared us righteous.

God demands perfection from us day by day or else we are damned. But because Christ is our perfection and meets God's demands for us, we can be free from the condemnation in our hearts. Twenty-four hours a day, Christ supplies what God demands.

Jesus, Thy blood and righteousness
my beauty are, my glorious dress.

—"Jesus Thy Blood and Righteousness"
by Nicolaus Zinzendorf

Do we now understand why Paul was so concerned with keeping the spring pure? To sneak works into the doctrine of salvation is to add diseased fungus to the pure water—it leads to uncertainty, defeat, and guilt. Faith in Christ alone is our only hope.

False teachers say faith in Christ *and* baptism are necessary for salvation. Faith in Christ *and* the sacraments are necessary. Faith in Christ *and*...you fill in the blank.

Whenever we add to the pure gospel, we dilute its message, deceive multitudes, and in the end, spread a spiritual disease among the people. Let's join Paul as a "keeper of the spring."

CHAPTER 3

THE RIGHT AND THE WRONG WAY

Several years ago, a friend told me a story about how he unintentionally found himself driving in the middle of a funeral procession. When he saw that the hearse was leaving the town to go to the cemetery, he knew he needed to turn around somewhere, so he turned off on a side road only to discover that dozens of cars continued to follow him. He stopped his own car, waiting along the side of the road, and watched as one by one the cars went by him. To this day he wonders where all those people finally ended up.

Whom you follow is incredibly important. To follow a leader who thinks he is right but is actually wrong might lead you to the gates of hell. Most people can recognize a bizarre false prophet, but the more subtle ones are difficult to detect.

The Apostle Paul wrote the book of Galatians to expose false teachers who were contaminating the gospel by mixing grace with works. Paul insisted that the issue was not what *we* do, but rather what *God has done.* We've shown that the gospel is a free gift from God, given independently of human merit. To believe differently is to follow the wrong leader. Christ said that the way to destruction was broad and "those who enter by it are many" (Matthew 7:13).

Even those who have received the free gift of salvation must be reminded of the daily application of the gospel message. For the faith that saves us is the faith within which we walk. We never outgrow our need for grace. As the songwriters Annie S. Hawks and Robert Lowry put it, "I need Thee every hour."

How do we know we are on the right road? In Galatians 3, the Apostle Paul gives three signposts to guide us. He pinpoints with even greater clarity what the good news of the gospel is all about.

SIGNPOST #1

First, the gospel, he says, is the work of the Holy Spirit, not the flesh. "O foolish Galatians! Who has bewitched you? It was before your eyes that Jesus Christ was publicly portrayed as crucified. Let me ask you only this: Did you receive the Spirit by works of the law or by hearing with faith? Are you so foolish? Having begun by the Spirit, are you now being perfected by the flesh?" (Galatians 3:1–3).

Did you get the contrast? The Holy Spirit was received

by faith; to be "born according to the Spirit" (Galatians 4:29) is a gift of God given to those who realize their helplessness and trust Christ alone. When we are born again, we become complete in Christ. Just as a baby is born complete with all physical characteristics with only the need to grow, so we, too, are born into God's family. That is a work of the Holy Spirit.

We are saved by faith and we are sanctified by faith. Our walk with God is not dependent on the flesh. Works have their place, but they can never bring spiritual victory to our lives. Only Christ can do that in response to faith. "Therefore, as you received Christ Jesus the Lord, so walk in him" (Colossians 2:6). The first signpost that assures us we are on the right road is the conviction that salvation is a work of the Holy Spirit, not of fleshly effort or sacraments.

SIGNPOST #2

Second, Paul says that the gospel is *a matter of faith, not Law.* "Just as Abraham 'believed God, and it was counted to him as righteousness'" (Galatians 3:6). Christ reminded the Pharisees, who prided themselves in their ancestry, that Abraham has no spiritual grandchildren.

No one is a Christian because he is born into the right family. Though physically the Jews might have been able to trace their pedigree back to Abraham, spiritually speaking, Christ said to them, "You are of your father the devil"

(John 8:44). Personal faith, individual faith, is needed for the gift of righteousness.

To try to be saved because of ancestry or through the Law only brings a curse. To quote Paul, "For all who rely on works of the law are under a curse; for it is written, 'Cursed be everyone who does not abide by all things written in the Book of the Law, and do them.' Now it is evident that no one is justified before God by the law, for 'The righteous shall live by faith'" (Galatians 3:10–11).

Thankfully, Paul says Christ was made a curse for us through "hanging on a tree" (3:13). To be stoned was humiliating, but stoning had a touch of dignity when compared to the shame of being crucified naked, lifted up for all to see. Paul's point was that Christ was shamefully treated and exposed, but He did it for us—He did it to "redeem us from the curse of the law" (3:13). Once again, the point is clear: Christ took our place, paid our penalty, and set us free.

The Law was like a plumb line that showed us we were crooked, but it could not straighten us out. "For by works of the law no human being will be justified in his sight, since through the law comes knowledge of sin" (Romans 3:20).

The second signpost that assures us that we have understood the gospel correctly is that we are saved by faith, not through the Law.

SIGNPOST #3

Third, Paul emphasizes that salvation is a matter of grace, not works. God does it all; we rest in His free gift on our behalf.

Think of the implications of grace!

Christ meets the demands of the Law for us every day. We often say we are "free from the law" (Romans 8:2) and this is true, of course. But what do we mean by this? Does it mean that God has withdrawn His need for righteousness? Has He become more lenient throughout the centuries and hence less demanding than He was in the Old Testament?

Let me state boldly that the Law has not been set aside; it continues to make incredible demands upon us—moment by moment, hour by hour, day by day, year by year. Indeed, if the Law had been set aside, Christ would not have had to die on the cross.

Here is the good news: although God demands perfection from me every day in order for me to receive His acceptance and approval, I personally do not need to meet those standards. Christ has come to save me; and He, as my representative in heaven, daily and hourly meets God's high standards. This sets me free from an impossible responsibility, namely, to satisfy the demands of a God whose holiness is beyond my comprehension.

Augustine, a great theologian and philosopher, was thrown into despair, contemplating his own failure to attain to the unspotted perfection of a holy God. Thankfully, he saw the corresponding truth—that thanks to Christ, he was off the hook. He cried out with both despair and joy, "Oh God, demand what you will but supply what you demand." It did not matter now how high God's standard was since he didn't have to meet it. What mattered is that he knew Christ had already met that standard for him. Every morning as he rose from the bed, every afternoon as he debated other scholars and wrote his books, Christ was continually Augustine's righteousness. Christ was meeting demands which, humanly speaking, are impossible and are beyond our ability to achieve.

Of course, there are certain *temporal* penalties that we need to pay for sins or crimes that we might commit. If you kill a person, you may have to spend the rest of your life in jail, perhaps even sentenced to death. If you hate a person, you will also have to pay the penalty that hatred brings with it. The temporal consequences of sin continue even after we are converted.

But Christ has redeemed us from the eternal penalty of our sin. Our place in heaven is assured, our rights before the throne uncontested. We enjoy a permanent standing in the sight of God and will understand the implications of this much better when we are personally ushered into the Divine Presence.

But what shall we do with the guilt that we still feel

within our restless conscience?

William Justice wrote, “For every failure to live up to some ‘ought,’ there is a tendency to punish oneself in such a way as to produce another failure. When I fail, I punish myself with more failure. I feel guilty, and thus feel the need to pay; but unfortunately, I choose a method that will leave me with a sense of having failed. On and on, the cycle rolls downward like a snowball rolling downhill adding to its weight and momentum with each revolution. The load of guilt becomes greater and greater, and the rate of descent faster and faster—this is the cycle of the damned” (*Guilt and Forgiveness,* Grand Rapids; Baker, 1980, p. 104).

What do we do with such an unrelenting sense of failure? The grace that saves us is the grace that keeps us. Just as I meet the divine standard by looking to Christ for my salvation, so must I respond to the residue of condemnation that still lurks in my heart. We can never defeat Satan’s accusations by convincing ourselves that we are not great sinners.

We must confront our sin realistically, but we must also look to the cross which was a *real* sacrifice for *real* sinners. Growth in grace is not about sinning less, it is seeing ourselves as more sinful than we think we are. The more we see ourselves as sinners, the more we look to the One who redeemed us and died in our stead.

Salvation is a package deal: we not only receive the gift

of righteousness through Christ, which is ours eternally, but we also receive the grace by which our consciences can be purified and we can walk with victory and joy. In addition, we receive the Holy Spirit who dwells within us as a companion and source of strength.

William Randolph Hearst, I am told, enjoyed famous paintings. He asked his staff to search for a specific piece, telling them he was willing to pay virtually any price for it. Later, as the story goes, they returned to tell him that they had indeed found the painting and he would not have to pay a single dime for it. It was found in his own warehouse!

When Christ redeemed us, many benefits were tucked away in the package we call *salvation.* Within our own warehouse, we have the privilege of finding unexpected blessings.

The biblical path is the way of the spirit, not the flesh; it is of faith, not Law; it is grace, not human merit. If we follow these signposts, we enter into the riches of the gospel.

CHAPTER 4

ADOPTED INTO GOD'S FAMILY

The American family is disintegrating before our eyes. Children have lost their sense of "belongingness;" they have not had the opportunity of growing up in a wholesome, emotionally supportive environment. It is difficult to live without love and value, a sense of purpose and meaning. These are shattered when we don't have roots or when we grow up in a strife-torn family.

Yet, we have an even greater need than a wholesome earthly family; we need God more than we need caring parents. As David said, "For my father and my mother have forsaken me, but the LORD will take me in" (Psalm 27:10). It's the difference between eternity and time; the difference between an Everlasting Father and a flawed human one.

We've all seen pictures of starving children around the world, and I hope that we are able to weep over the emotional and spiritual pain that engulfs our globe. And yet, though it is difficult for me to say this, it is better to be a child starving in Africa who will go to heaven, than to be a pampered adult in the United States who will end up in hell. Unfortunately, we sometimes live as though this is the only world that ever will be; but we weren't created for this world—we were created for the invisible world to come. Our relationship with Jesus Christ determines our eternal destiny.

Paul wrote the book of Galatians to answer the question of how a sinner can be right with God. Previously, I emphasized the doctrine of justification: to be declared righteous by God. This is a gift of grace, it does not come through the Law nor through works. Nobody has ever made it to heaven by trying to be as good as somebody else! Only the perfect can enter, and therefore, we must be accepted on the basis of Christ.

THE SONSHIP OF ISRAEL

To illustrate the difference between Law and grace, and to show how radically we are blessed once we are justified, Paul teaches that we are sons of God. He contrasts this with the nation Israel, which he says was like a child. "I mean that the heir, as long as he is a child, is no different from a slave, though he is the owner of everything, but he is under guardians and managers until the date set by his father" (Galatians 4:1, 2). Paul's point is that though a child might have great wealth, he is no better off than a slave as long as he (the child) is too young to enjoy his inheritance. In the same way, Israel was really a child, promised great wealth but too "young" to enjoy that wealth.

In the ancient world there was a much sharper division between adults and children than exists in our own society. When Paul says that Israel was like a child (Galatians 4:1–4), he meant that the nation had not grown up. Like a child, the nation had limited understanding; the people did not see Christ clearly, and their knowledge of God and His relationship to the world was restricted. Children are not able to see "the big picture." They are caught up with details, missing the significance of what they are doing.

Children also have limited privileges. Israel, under the Law, was not able to communicate directly with God in the Holy of Holies, therefore the priesthood was instituted. There were many regulations and often there was not a clear picture of spiritual freedom and the blessings of forgiveness. The promises were there but their fulfillment seemed afar off.

So, says Paul, Israel was a child destined to inherit great blessings, but the nation actually enjoyed little of its privileges. It was more like a slave than a son.

OUR SONSHIP

Then God entered the picture! "But when the fullness of time had come, God sent forth his Son, born of woman, born under the law" (Galatians 4:4). With the coming of Christ, everything changed. The child now stood to inherit the blessings. The wealth which had been stored up could finally be used. The slave could live like a son.

Now, says Paul, all believers in Christ are sons. "To redeem those who were under the law, so that we might receive adoption as sons. And because you are sons, God has sent the Spirit of his Son into our hearts, crying, 'Abba! Father!'" (Galatians 4:5–6).

Christ's assignment was specific: to redeem us. That is, He, as the Son of God, came to give a sacrifice of infinite value that we might be freed from the bondage of sin and the Law. With sixty million slaves in the Roman Empire, this imagery was well-known in Paul's day—the purchase and trade of slaves happened continuously.

If a man owned a slave, that slave could either be freed or adopted into the family as a son. This adoption meant that the new son had all the rights of a legitimate son. His previous debts were cancelled; he was given all the rights and honors that pertained to adoption. In the same way, through Christ we have been adopted into God's family and given sonship status. We have such intimacy with Him that we can cry, "Abba! Father!" a term of endearment, a term that signifies close family bonding.

Let's not miss Paul's point: a person who is saved today is not like a child who has to grow into his inheritance—

he is instantly considered by God to be a son with all established rights, privileges, and advantages. We become God's children through regeneration and are instantly elevated to the full status of sons.

A new believer, one so new to the faith that he scarcely knows the difference between the Old and New Testaments has the same advantages, the same rights and privileges as those who have been saved for many, many years. We don't have to wait to receive our inheritance, we possess it through faith the moment we believe.

THE IMPLICATIONS OF SONSHIP

What are the implications of sonship for us? First, our new Father bears responsibility for His children. He will not abandon us. He will not put us up for adoption; we will never be lost in a child custody battle. We may disobey Him, for which He will discipline us, but He will never cast us aside.

Second, we are loved unconditionally. It would be heresy to say that God would love us more if only we were better. There is nothing that we can do to make ourselves more pleasing in His sight. We must view ourselves as complete in Christ and belonging to Him forever. We are not loved of ourselves, we are loved because of Him.

Third, our heavenly family is more important than our earthly family. I am not saying that the trauma of a dysfunctional family can be easily set aside; I'm not insisting that the abuses that go on in our homes can simply be ignored. Those who are thus wounded must work through these hurts as best they can, but they should do so knowing that there is an anchor in their life that will not let them drift aimlessly.

No matter how bad it is here, eternity will more than compensate for it. "For I consider that the sufferings of this present time are not worth comparing with the glory that is to be revealed to us" (Romans 8:18). No wonder Paul can say, "So you are no longer a slave, but a son, and if a son, then an heir through God" (Galatians 4:7).

A woman who was raised in an orphanage told me how she craved to be a part of a family. As a teenager she walked the streets in the evenings, straining to look through windows just to see a family together. She often saw them eating at a table or reclining in the living room. She would try to imagine what it would be like to really "belong." Finally at the age of 20, and after being mistreated at several foster homes, she met Christian parents who told her, "Don't call us Mr. and Mrs.…it's Mom and Dad." She was thrilled. At last the formalities of merely being an acquaintance were past; she moved right into the intimacy of the family circle.

Yes, we presently are sons, and the day is coming when we will receive our inheritance in full. "And if children, then heirs—heirs of God and fellow heirs with Christ" (Romans 8:17a). We shall even share in His eternal glory. No, we will never become like God, for He is beyond all human limitations. But He is generous enough to honor us as a father honors his children.

"See what kind of love the Father has given to us, that we should be called children of God; and so we are. The reason why the world does not know us is that it did not know him. Beloved, we are God's children now, and what we will be has not yet appeared; but we know that when he appears we shall be like him, because we shall see him as he is" (1 John 3:1–2).

In what sense shall we be like Christ? We shall have a similar body—a glorified body that is not subject to the limitations of matter, a body that is indestructible. We shall have similar desires for holiness, purity, and appreciation for God the Father. And of course, we share a similar future, being together forever in the presence of God the Father, seated at His right hand. The riches of sonship!

My Father is rich in houses and lands,
He holdeth the wealth of the world in His hands!
Of rubies and diamonds, of silver and gold,
His coffers are full, He has riches untold.
I'm a child of the King,
A child of the King:

With Jesus my Savior,
I'm a child of the King.

—"A Child of the King"
by Harriet E. Buell

The gospel does not just get us to heaven. It gives us the *wealth* of heaven. Best of all, it makes us children of our Heavenly Father; Christ is our brother, and other believers are intimate relatives of the same family.

CHAPTER 5

ENJOY YOUR FREEDOM

Here is an assignment: take a moment to write down all the things you think would make you holy. I'm sure that most of us would include memorizing Scripture, praying, witnessing, and perhaps even selling our "goods to feed the poor" (1 Corinthians 13:3 KJV).

Now I'd like you to mentally list all the things that would make you happy. Perhaps you would like a better spouse, better health, more money, a vacation, or a peaceful environment.

Paul would tell us that none of these lifestyles truly reflect where "life is at." He writes, "For in Christ Jesus neither circumcision nor uncircumcision counts for anything, but only faith working through love" (Galatians 5:6).

Circumcision is used in this verse as a symbol of the entire Jewish religion. It represents the lifestyle of people who worked hard to be holy. If you were to ask the Jews to make a list of the things that would make them holy, it would be a long list indeed. For the law was complex and included detailed matters that pertained to every facet of their existence. Many Jews tried to keep these regulations meticulously. There was little joy and lots of work.

The word *un*circumcision used here refers to the Greeks who glorified the human body and emphasized a life of indulgence. To them, circumcision was a sign of shame; those who participated in the ancient Olympic Games had to prove that they weren't circumcised. Here the word represents a lifestyle of sensuality, aesthetic beauty, and human attainment. If you asked a Greek what it would take to be happy, his list would have included virtually all of the pleasures that the world had to offer.

Interestingly, Paul says that both lifestyles amount to nothing. Let's look at them now in more detail.

THE WAY OF RELIGION

First of all, the way of religion is a way of rituals, human discipline, and various kinds of works-based righteousness. "Look: I, Paul, say to you that if you accept circumcision, Christ will be of no advantage to you. I testify again to every man who accepts circumcision that he is obligated to keep the whole law" (Galatians 5:2–3).

Paul's point is this: just as it is wrong to think that we are saved by works, so it is wrong to think that we are sanctified by works! If we think we are saved by works, we diminish the cross; if we think that sanctification (personal victory) comes through our human efforts, we again diminish what Christ has done for us. Christ's provision included the gift of our justification as well as the gift of our sanctification. Both come to us by faith.

If you are a perfectionist, you will gravitate toward works-based righteousness. You will find a certain sense of satisfaction in putting yourself under the law of whatever variety, and you will also demand that others be there with you. Unfortunately, perfectionists often feel frustrated, unable to enjoy the company of those who are not trying as hard as they are. Their bar is always raised a notch higher until most perfectionists fall back in despair. No matter how hard they work, holiness seems completely beyond reach.

Paul speaks of those who want to be sanctified through works as being "severed from Christ...fallen away from grace" (Galatians 5:4). This doesn't mean that they have lost their salvation, but rather Christ is of no benefit to them in their daily walk—they are cut off from Christ's power. All of us have met Christians who have said, "I want to witness, but I have nothing to say because Christ seems to be of no benefit to me."

To summarize: if we think that holiness is just a matter of memorizing Scripture, praying, and the spiritual disciplines, we will never measure up; there will be little joy. We will experience the grind but not the glory.

Legalists can be vicious with one another. Paul writes, "But if you bite and devour one another, watch out that you are not consumed by one another" (Galatians 5:15). Legalists become meticulous judges of the behavior of other people. Having defined the Christian life in terms of external effort, they are critical of all those who do not fall into their particular mold. To become righteous by observing rules, however good these rules might be, is to experience frustration and the feeling that one has never done enough.

THE WAY OF HAPPINESS

We come now to the way of happiness, the Greek interpretation of the "good life." I mentioned that the Greeks were into pleasure; they believed that religion was confining and quite contrary to happiness. Young Christians who become discouraged often say, in effect, "I'm going to trade holiness for happiness. I will satisfy my own desires; I will do my own thing, and I will enjoy what I think is right for me." They plunge headlong into a life of ease and indulgence which often leads to a fleshly, self-centered existence.

The indulgence of the flesh is slavery. The more we feed our fleshly desires, the stronger they become. Take any area of the flesh and, no matter how appealing it might be, that particular weakness can ultimately consume any one of us. The flesh always hungers for more fulfillment and always demands more than we are ever able to give.

To choose the so-called way of happiness creates vacillation and guilt in the life of a Christian. Despair leads to more guilt; the guilt, in turn, magnifies the despair. Though he does whatever he feels like doing, the pleasure-seeker is robbed of happiness. He has a raging civil war within and he doesn't know how to negotiate a peace treaty. That's why embarking on the life of the flesh usually ends with alcoholism, immorality, or drug abuse. People are trying to deaden the pain of an empty life.

If the so-called path to holiness leads nowhere, and the path to happiness is fraught with dangers and despair, where should we turn? To quote Paul once again, "For in Christ Jesus neither circumcision nor uncircumcision counts for anything, but only faith working through love" (Galatians 5:6).

Thankfully, there is a way. Paul says the answer is "faith working through love."

FAITH WORKING THROUGH LOVE

Faith, according to Paul, is the answer for the person who seeks holiness as well as for the person who seeks happiness. In other words, holiness and happiness are attained by resting in what God has done; it is the kind of faith that enjoys the righteousness and holiness that is already ours in Jesus Christ. Holiness can never be attained by looking to our good works, however well-intentioned they may be, but by looking to Christ and drawing from Him the resources that are at our disposal because of who we are in Him.

What role do the Christian disciplines play in our lives? Obviously, it is important to memorize Scripture, to pray, to yield, and to read and study the Bible. These works are of value in our pursuit of holiness to the extent that they expand our understanding of what God has done for us. The point is that in and of themselves, such efforts have no power to change us. These disciplines bring about a transformation only when they point beyond themselves to the righteousness and glory of Christ. It is not what we do that makes us holy; it is the *direction of our focus,* the direction of our faith and love.

Every day we need a fresh understanding of Christ and what He has done for us. Every day we need to affirm the promises of the Lord, to choose to walk in the Spirit and not fulfill the desires of the flesh. But it is a walk of faith; it is a walk that draws on resources that have already been given us in Jesus Christ.

One day I met a couple who told me that they were having conflict in their marriage. So they decided to memorize more verses of Scripture, to pray more, and to exercise the disciplines of the faith. Incredibly, along with such well-intentioned efforts, their arguments escalated.

There was nothing they could do that would seem to relieve the tension.

Then they read Galatians 5:6 this way, "For in Christ Jesus neither being happily married nor being unhappily married means anything, but faith working through love." When they began to focus on who they were in Christ and the completeness of His work, they were then free to finally be honest with each other so that they could seriously address the differences between them.

Someone has suggested that Galatians 5:6 can be an "idol smasher" if read this way: "For neither being promoted nor being passed over for a promotion means anything; neither having money nor not having money means anything; neither having a happy marriage nor an unhappy marriage means anything—all these idols are unimportant but what is essential is 'faith working through love.'"

The faith that saved us is the same faith with which we walk. *And once we have found the route to holiness, we have also found the route to happiness.* For the same faith that makes us holy also makes us happy.

Perhaps God wants to free you today from the bondage of a critical spirit, a kind of legalism that assesses other Christians by external rules. The rules may be important just like foul lines on a basketball court tell us where the boundaries are, but those rules cannot create the fruit of the Spirit. "Faith working through love" is the key that unlocks the door to both holiness and happiness.

CHAPTER 6

CONFLICT WITHIN THE SOUL

Back in 1991, a video showing Rodney King being beaten during an arrest was replayed many times on news channels throughout the United States. Every time King tried to stand up, he was beaten back down. He wasn't even allowed to crawl without being hit with a baton.

What a picture of the conflict of the soul! I remember speaking to a young man who had fathered a child and now his girlfriend wouldn't let him see his own daughter. Though the man was a Christian, he was so overtaken with guilt, grief, and despair that it appeared as if he would never be able to walk with his head held high again.

I think of those who are overcome with addictions, those who are slaves to pornography, alcohol, or drugs. No matter how many promises are made, they are always broken. What does the Bible have to say to believers caught in such sins?

WE MUST LEARN TO STAND

Paul writes, "For freedom Christ has set us free; stand firm therefore, and do not submit again to a yoke of slavery" (Galatians 5:1). But how can we as sinners stand before God; and after being knocked down, how do we get up again—and continue to stand?

We must return to the theme of Galatians: we are declared righteous by God when we place our trust in Christ alone. Righteousness is a gift that can be applied to any sinner regardless of his sins and crimes.

Of course, Christ's righteousness is a permanent gift that has paid the debt of our sins—past, present, and future. That's what Paul means when he says we are "in Christ." Even when we struggle with the flesh and lose, Christ is still our righteousness. That's why we can keep standing. Christ is our representative before God. It is the fact of our acceptance in Him that allows us to stand up when we fall.

Before the throne my Surety stands;
My name is written on His hands.

—"Five Bleeding Wounds He Bears"
by Charles Wesley

Thus, when faced with sin and failure, our responsibility is to remember that Christ continually represents us to

God the Father, and that His righteousness, given to us, is all we need.

But what do we do when we are overwhelmed by our sins? George Spalatin, a co-worker of Martin Luther, had given a friend some advice which he later came to regard as sinful. He was immersed in grief and could not be consoled.

When Luther learned of Spalatin's grief, he didn't try to minimize the sin, rather, he magnified grace. In a letter dated August 21, 1544, he wrote:

> *"My faithful request and admonition is that you join our company and associate with us who are real, great and hard-boiled sinners. You must by no means make Christ to seem paltry and trifling to us as though He could be our helper only when we want to be rid from imaginary, nominal and childish sins. No, no! That would not be good for us. He must rather be a savior and redeemer from real, great, grievous, and damnable transgressions and iniquities, yea from the very greatest and most shocking sins; to be brief, from all sins added together in a grand total...You will have to get used to the belief that Christ is a real savior and you a real sinner. For God is neither jesting nor dealing in imaginary affairs. But He was greatly and most assuredly in earnest when He sent his own Son into the world and sacrificed Him for our sakes."*

Yes, we need a gospel that is able to save great, hard-boiled sinners. There is no use trying to minimize our sin or to "reeducate" our conscience so that we can cope with guilt. No, we must realize that Jesus Christ died for real sinners, even those who have committed "damnable transgressions."

Paul says that we should no longer "submit again to a yoke of slavery" but stand in the freedom of Christ. The "yoke of slavery" refers to looking to ourselves to find some reason why God should accept us or some reason why He should forgive us. Sometimes we do this by making a promise that we shall never commit the same sin again, or we try to think back to times when we did obey God. There are also many people who live with guilt, assuming that guilt is punishment by God. All such attempts to establish a relationship with God are futile and greatly encouraged by the devil.

We must not meet the accusations of our conscience by either minimizing the sin or trying to look to something we have done to make ourselves feel better. No, every time we sin we must reaffirm that our acceptance before God has remained unchanged because of the work of Christ on our behalf.

To quote Paul, "Who shall bring any charge against God's elect? It is God who justifies. Who is to condemn? Christ Jesus is the one who died—more than that, who was raised—who is at the right hand of God, who indeed is interceding for us" (Romans 8:33–34).

How do we stand up? Through faith in Christ's complete work on our behalf. We stand because we know we have been completely received by our Heavenly Father independently of any works that we could perform, independently of what we deserve. And when we fall, we cling to the same truth and find comfort in knowing that our acceptance before God has remained unchanged.

WE MUST LEARN TO WALK

Second, after we have learned to stand, we should begin to walk. Specifically, Paul says, "But I say, walk by the Spirit, and you will not gratify the desires of the flesh" (Galatians 5:16). We are tempted to read the verse this way: "But I say stop carrying out the desires of the flesh and you will walk in the Spirit."

Paul, of course, reverses the order. He knows that we need the fullness of the Spirit up front, even before we can begin to say "no" to the flesh or walk in the strength of a yielded life. That's why the Holy Spirit indwells every believer—He is available at the very beginning of the Christian life. New Christians, carnal Christians, and those of us who have desired the will of God for many years—all of us—must learn to walk in the Spirit.

How is this done? By faith. Just as we put our faith in

Christ for our acceptance before God, we must exercise the same faith in the power of the Holy Spirit.

The famous preacher F.B. Meyer tells about the time he struggled with the filling of the Holy Spirit. Though he had wept at many altars and, through yieldedness, sought some kind of special infilling, it simply never seemed to happen. Then in his weariness he prayed, "Oh Lord, you know that no one needs the filling of the Holy Spirit more than I. Yet, I am too tired to agonize, I am too weary to seek it." Just then, he says, it was as if he heard the voice of the Holy Spirit say, "Just as you have received salvation from the Christ of the cross, in the same way, receive the fullness of the Spirit from the Christ of the resurrection." So he began to drink of the Spirit's fullness in faith. And in his words, "I have been drinking ever since."

The fullness of the Spirit is *not a reward* for good behavior; the Spirit is given to us as sinners so that we might experience good behavior.

The cross enables us to stand and to remain standing; but it is the Spirit who helps us walk in the Christian life. As we appropriate the Spirit's power by faith, we will find that we don't fall as often.

WE MUST LEARN TO FIGHT

Next, Paul tells us that we should keep fighting. "For the desires of the flesh are against the Spirit, and the desires of the Spirit are against the flesh, for these are opposed to each other, to keep you from doing the things you want to do" (Galatians 5:17). Though Paul doesn't say it here, in Ephesians 6 he refers to us as fighting with the swordof the Spirit "which is the word of God."

All of us know the fight that goes on between the flesh and the Spirit, each desiring supremacy in our lives. These two forces are bitter enemies and each seeks to dominate the other. Paul speaks about the works of the flesh and gives a long catalog of sins, each wanting to take hold in our lives.

Here is hope for everyone! As I conclude these brief thoughts on Galatians, I am reminded of a letter I received from a rapist serving time in prison for raping four women. He wrote, "I have been able to leave my past behind, but my victims have not. It hurts me to be joyous and yet I cannot help them. How can I make amends for those who were my victims? It was sheer terror for me to be under the pressures of sin and addictions for the first one-half century of my life. Since being born again, God has put me through heat—He has turned up the thermostat. When I go through one of those glazing experiences, I forget His ability to get me through. But I'm learning."

Do we have a gospel that is able to save a rapist? The answer, of course, is *yes.* Christ died for sinners—*real* sinners.

He, too, can stand cleansed by Christ, walk in the Spirit's fullness, and fight by using God's Word. He must stand in the freedom with which Christ made him free.

God has declared us to be righteous; we are accepted in the Beloved One. In light of that, we can rejoice in our perfect standing. My friend, no matter how far you have fallen, if you believe in Christ alone, He will declare you righteous. He will enable you to *stand* then *walk* then *fight.*

Yes, we can make it—living for Christ all the way en route to our heavenly city.

51042960R00033

Made in the USA
Columbia, SC
15 February 2019